MW00875563

THIS LOG BELONGS TO

Ashlie Tsair

ADDRESS   1297

EMAIL

PHONE

Copyright ©
All rights reserved. No part of this publication may be reproduced, distributed,
or transmitted in any form or by any means, including photocopying, recording,
or other electronic or mechanical methods, without the prior written permission
of the publisher, except in the case of brief quotations embodied in critical reviews
and certain other noncommercial uses permitted by copyright law.

CONTENTS

CONTENTS

CONTENTS

CLIENT NAME

DATE

PHONE

EMAIL

LOOK / OCCASION

SKIN

PRIMER

FOUNDATION

CONCEALER

POWDER

HIGHLIGHTER

CONTOUR

BLUSH

EYES

BROW BONE

LID

CREASE

UNDER EYE

EYELINER

MASCARA

BROW

LIPS

LIP LINER

LIPSTICK

GLOSS

NOTES / INSPIRATION

KEY PRODUCTS AND TOOLS

CLIENT NAME

DATE

PHONE

EMAIL

LOOK / OCCASION

SKIN

PRIMER

FOUNDATION

CONCEALER

POWDER

HIGHLIGHTER

CONTOUR

BLUSH

EYES

BROW BONE

LID

CREASE

UNDER EYE

EYELINER

MASCARA

BROW

LIPS

LIP LINER

LIPSTICK

GLOSS

KEY PRODUCTS AND TOOLS

NOTES / INSPIRATION

4

CLIENT NAME

DATE

PHONE

EMAIL

LOOK / OCCASION

SKIN

PRIMER

FOUNDATION

CONCEALER

POWDER

HIGHLIGHTER

CONTOUR

BLUSH

EYES

BROW BONE

LID

CREASE

UNDER EYE

EYELINER

MASCARA

BROW

LIPS

LIP LINER

LIPSTICK

GLOSS

NOTES / INSPIRATION

KEY PRODUCTS AND TOOLS

CLIENT NAME

DATE

PHONE

EMAIL

LOOK / OCCASION

SKIN

PRIMER

FOUNDATION

CONCEALER

POWDER

HIGHLIGHTER

CONTOUR

BLUSH

EYES

BROW BONE

LID

CREASE

UNDER EYE

EYELINER

MASCARA

BROW

LIPS

LIP LINER

LIPSTICK

GLOSS

NOTES / INSPIRATION

KEY PRODUCTS AND TOOLS

CLIENT NAME

DATE

PHONE

EMAIL

LOOK / OCCASION

SKIN

PRIMER

FOUNDATION

CONCEALER

POWDER

HIGHLIGHTER

CONTOUR

BLUSH

EYES

BROW BONE

LID

CREASE

UNDER EYE

EYELINER

MASCARA

BROW

LIPS

LIP LINER

LIPSTICK

GLOSS

NOTES / INSPIRATION

KEY PRODUCTS AND TOOLS

CLIENT NAME

DATE

PHONE

EMAIL

LOOK / OCCASION

SKIN

PRIMER

FOUNDATION

CONCEALER

POWDER

HIGHLIGHTER

CONTOUR

BLUSH

EYES

BROW BONE

LID

CREASE

UNDER EYE

EYELINER

MASCARA

BROW

LIPS

LIP LINER

LIPSTICK

GLOSS

NOTES / INSPIRATION

KEY PRODUCTS AND TOOLS

CLIENT NAME

DATE

PHONE

EMAIL

LOOK / OCCASION

SKIN

PRIMER

FOUNDATION

CONCEALER

POWDER

HIGHLIGHTER

CONTOUR

BLUSH

EYES

BROW BONE

LID

CREASE

UNDER EYE

EYELINER

MASCARA

BROW

LIPS

LIP LINER

LIPSTICK

GLOSS

KEY PRODUCTS AND TOOLS

NOTES / INSPIRATION

CLIENT NAME

DATE

PHONE

EMAIL

LOOK / OCCASION

SKIN

PRIMER

FOUNDATION

CONCEALER

POWDER

HIGHLIGHTER

CONTOUR

BLUSH

EYES

BROW BONE

LID

CREASE

UNDER EYE

EYELINER

MASCARA

BROW

LIPS

LIP LINER

LIPSTICK

GLOSS

KEY PRODUCTS AND TOOLS

NOTES / INSPIRATION

CLIENT NAME

DATE

PHONE

EMAIL

LOOK / OCCASION

SKIN

PRIMER

FOUNDATION

CONCEALER

POWDER

HIGHLIGHTER

CONTOUR

BLUSH

EYES

BROW BONE

LID

CREASE

UNDER EYE

EYELINER

MASCARA

BROW

LIPS

LIP LINER

LIPSTICK

GLOSS

NOTES / INSPIRATION

KEY PRODUCTS AND TOOLS

18

CLIENT NAME

DATE

PHONE

EMAIL

LOOK / OCCASION

SKIN

PRIMER

FOUNDATION

CONCEALER

POWDER

HIGHLIGHTER

CONTOUR

BLUSH

EYES

BROW BONE

LID

CREASE

UNDER EYE

EYELINER

MASCARA

BROW

LIPS

LIP LINER

LIPSTICK

GLOSS

NOTES / INSPIRATION

KEY PRODUCTS AND TOOLS

CLIENT NAME

DATE

PHONE

EMAIL

LOOK / OCCASION

SKIN

PRIMER

FOUNDATION

CONCEALER

POWDER

HIGHLIGHTER

CONTOUR

BLUSH

EYES

BROW BONE

LID

CREASE

UNDER EYE

EYELINER

MASCARA

BROW

LIPS

LIP LINER

LIPSTICK

GLOSS

NOTES / INSPIRATION

KEY PRODUCTS AND TOOLS

CLIENT NAME

DATE _____

PHONE _____

EMAIL _____

LOOK / OCCASION _____

SKIN

PRIMER _____

FOUNDATION _____

CONCEALER _____

POWDER _____

HIGHLIGHTER _____

CONTOUR _____

BLUSH _____

EYES

BROW BONE _____

LID _____

CREASE _____

UNDER EYE _____

EYELINER _____

MASCARA _____

BROW _____

LIPS

LIP LINER _____

LIPSTICK _____

GLOSS _____

KEY PRODUCTS AND TOOLS

NOTES / INSPIRATION

CLIENT NAME

DATE

PHONE

EMAIL

LOOK / OCCASION

SKIN

PRIMER

FOUNDATION

CONCEALER

POWDER

HIGHLIGHTER

CONTOUR

BLUSH

EYES

BROW BONE

LID

CREASE

UNDER EYE

EYELINER

MASCARA

BROW

LIPS

LIP LINER

LIPSTICK

GLOSS

NOTES / INSPIRATION

KEY PRODUCTS AND TOOLS

CLIENT NAME

DATE

PHONE

EMAIL

LOOK / OCCASION

SKIN

PRIMER

FOUNDATION

CONCEALER

POWDER

HIGHLIGHTER

CONTOUR

BLUSH

EYES

BROW BONE

LID

CREASE

UNDER EYE

EYELINER

MASCARA

BROW

LIPS

LIP LINER

LIPSTICK

GLOSS

NOTES / INSPIRATION

KEY PRODUCTS AND TOOLS

CLIENT NAME

DATE _____

PHONE _____

EMAIL _____

LOOK / OCCASION _____

SKIN

PRIMER _____

FOUNDATION _____

CONCEALER _____

POWDER _____

HIGHLIGHTER _____

CONTOUR _____

BLUSH _____

EYES

BROW BONE _____

LID _____

CREASE _____

UNDER EYE _____

EYELINER _____

MASCARA _____

BROW _____

LIPS

LIP LINER _____

LIPSTICK _____

GLOSS _____

KEY PRODUCTS AND TOOLS

NOTES / INSPIRATION

CLIENT NAME

DATE

PHONE

EMAIL

LOOK / OCCASION

SKIN

PRIMER

FOUNDATION

CONCEALER

POWDER

HIGHLIGHTER

CONTOUR

BLUSH

EYES

BROW BONE

LID

CREASE

UNDER EYE

EYELINER

MASCARA

BROW

LIPS

LIP LINER

LIPSTICK

GLOSS

KEY PRODUCTS AND TOOLS

NOTES / INSPIRATION

CLIENT NAME

DATE

PHONE

EMAIL

LOOK / OCCASION

SKIN

PRIMER

FOUNDATION

CONCEALER

POWDER

HIGHLIGHTER

CONTOUR

BLUSH

EYES

BROW BONE

LID

CREASE

UNDER EYE

EYELINER

MASCARA

BROW

LIPS

LIP LINER

LIPSTICK

GLOSS

KEY PRODUCTS AND TOOLS

NOTES / INSPIRATION

CLIENT NAME

DATE

PHONE

EMAIL

LOOK / OCCASION

SKIN

PRIMER

FOUNDATION

CONCEALER

POWDER

HIGHLIGHTER

CONTOUR

BLUSH

EYES

BROW BONE

LID

CREASE

UNDER EYE

EYELINER

MASCARA

BROW

LIPS

LIP LINER

LIPSTICK

GLOSS

NOTES / INSPIRATION

KEY PRODUCTS AND TOOLS

CLIENT NAME

DATE

PHONE

EMAIL

LOOK / OCCASION

SKIN

PRIMER

FOUNDATION

CONCEALER

POWDER

HIGHLIGHTER

CONTOUR

BLUSH

EYES

BROW BONE

LID

CREASE

UNDER EYE

EYELINER

MASCARA

BROW

LIPS

LIP LINER

LIPSTICK

GLOSS

KEY PRODUCTS AND TOOLS

NOTES / INSPIRATION

CLIENT NAME

DATE

PHONE

EMAIL

LOOK / OCCASION

SKIN

PRIMER

FOUNDATION

CONCEALER

POWDER

HIGHLIGHTER

CONTOUR

BLUSH

EYES

BROW BONE

LID

CREASE

UNDER EYE

EYELINER

MASCARA

BROW

LIPS

LIP LINER

LIPSTICK

GLOSS

KEY PRODUCTS AND TOOLS

NOTES / INSPIRATION

CLIENT NAME

DATE

PHONE

EMAIL

LOOK / OCCASION

SKIN

PRIMER

FOUNDATION

CONCEALER

POWDER

HIGHLIGHTER

CONTOUR

BLUSH

EYES

BROW BONE

LID

CREASE

UNDER EYE

EYELINER

MASCARA

BROW

LIPS

LIP LINER

LIPSTICK

GLOSS

NOTES / INSPIRATION

KEY PRODUCTS AND TOOLS

CLIENT NAME

DATE

PHONE

EMAIL

LOOK / OCCASION

SKIN

PRIMER

FOUNDATION

CONCEALER

POWDER

HIGHLIGHTER

CONTOUR

BLUSH

EYES

BROW BONE

LID

CREASE

UNDER EYE

EYELINER

MASCARA

BROW

LIPS

LIP LINER

LIPSTICK

GLOSS

NOTES / INSPIRATION

KEY PRODUCTS AND TOOLS

CLIENT NAME

DATE

PHONE

EMAIL

LOOK / OCCASION

SKIN

PRIMER

FOUNDATION

CONCEALER

POWDER

HIGHLIGHTER

CONTOUR

BLUSH

EYES

BROW BONE

LID

CREASE

UNDER EYE

EYELINER

MASCARA

BROW

LIPS

LIP LINER

LIPSTICK

GLOSS

NOTES / INSPIRATION

KEY PRODUCTS AND TOOLS

CLIENT NAME

DATE

PHONE

EMAIL

LOOK / OCCASION

SKIN

PRIMER

FOUNDATION

CONCEALER

POWDER

HIGHLIGHTER

CONTOUR

BLUSH

EYES

BROW BONE

LID

CREASE

UNDER EYE

EYELINER

MASCARA

BROW

LIPS

LIP LINER

LIPSTICK

GLOSS

NOTES / INSPIRATION

KEY PRODUCTS AND TOOLS

CLIENT NAME

DATE

PHONE

EMAIL

LOOK / OCCASION

SKIN

PRIMER

FOUNDATION

CONCEALER

POWDER

HIGHLIGHTER

CONTOUR

BLUSH

EYES

BROW BONE

LID

CREASE

UNDER EYE

EYELINER

MASCARA

BROW

LIPS

LIP LINER

LIPSTICK

GLOSS

KEY PRODUCTS AND TOOLS

NOTES / INSPIRATION

CLIENT NAME

DATE

PHONE

EMAIL

LOOK / OCCASION

SKIN

PRIMER

FOUNDATION

CONCEALER

POWDER

HIGHLIGHTER

CONTOUR

BLUSH

EYES

BROW BONE

LID

CREASE

UNDER EYE

EYELINER

MASCARA

BROW

LIPS

LIP LINER

LIPSTICK

GLOSS

NOTES / INSPIRATION

KEY PRODUCTS AND TOOLS

CLIENT NAME

DATE

PHONE

EMAIL

LOOK / OCCASION

SKIN

PRIMER

FOUNDATION

CONCEALER

POWDER

HIGHLIGHTER

CONTOUR

BLUSH

EYES

BROW BONE

LID

CREASE

UNDER EYE

EYELINER

MASCARA

BROW

LIPS

LIP LINER

LIPSTICK

GLOSS

NOTES / INSPIRATION

KEY PRODUCTS AND TOOLS

54

CLIENT NAME

DATE

PHONE

EMAIL

LOOK / OCCASION

SKIN

PRIMER

FOUNDATION

CONCEALER

POWDER

HIGHLIGHTER

CONTOUR

BLUSH

EYES

BROW BONE

LID

CREASE

UNDER EYE

EYELINER

MASCARA

BROW

LIPS

LIP LINER

LIPSTICK

GLOSS

NOTES / INSPIRATION

KEY PRODUCTS AND TOOLS

CLIENT NAME

PHONE

EMAIL

LOOK / OCCASION

SKIN

PRIMER

FOUNDATION

CONCEALER

POWDER

HIGHLIGHTER

CONTOUR

BLUSH

EYES

BROW BONE

LID

CREASE

UNDER EYE

EYELINER

MASCARA

BROW

LIPS

LIP LINER

LIPSTICK

GLOSS

NOTES / INSPIRATION

KEY PRODUCTS AND TOOLS

CLIENT NAME

DATE

PHONE

EMAIL

LOOK / OCCASION

SKIN

PRIMER

FOUNDATION

CONCEALER

POWDER

HIGHLIGHTER

CONTOUR

BLUSH

EYES

BROW BONE

LID

CREASE

UNDER EYE

EYELINER

MASCARA

BROW

LIPS

LIP LINER

LIPSTICK

GLOSS

NOTES / INSPIRATION

KEY PRODUCTS AND TOOLS

CLIENT NAME

DATE

PHONE

EMAIL

LOOK / OCCASION

SKIN

PRIMER

FOUNDATION

CONCEALER

POWDER

HIGHLIGHTER

CONTOUR

BLUSH

EYES

BROW BONE

LID

CREASE

UNDER EYE

EYELINER

MASCARA

BROW

LIPS

LIP LINER

LIPSTICK

GLOSS

NOTES / INSPIRATION

KEY PRODUCTS AND TOOLS

CLIENT NAME

DATE

PHONE

EMAIL

LOOK / OCCASION

SKIN

PRIMER

FOUNDATION

CONCEALER

POWDER

HIGHLIGHTER

CONTOUR

BLUSH

EYES

BROW BONE

LID

CREASE

UNDER EYE

EYELINER

MASCARA

BROW

LIPS

LIP LINER

LIPSTICK

GLOSS

KEY PRODUCTS AND TOOLS

NOTES / INSPIRATION

CLIENT NAME

DATE

PHONE

EMAIL

LOOK / OCCASION

SKIN

PRIMER

FOUNDATION

CONCEALER

POWDER

HIGHLIGHTER

CONTOUR

BLUSH

EYES

BROW BONE

LID

CREASE

UNDER EYE

EYELINER

MASCARA

BROW

LIPS

LIP LINER

LIPSTICK

GLOSS

KEY PRODUCTS AND TOOLS

NOTES / INSPIRATION

CLIENT NAME

DATE

PHONE

EMAIL

LOOK / OCCASION

SKIN

PRIMER

FOUNDATION

CONCEALER

POWDER

HIGHLIGHTER

CONTOUR

BLUSH

EYES

BROW BONE

LID

CREASE

UNDER EYE

EYELINER

MASCARA

BROW

LIPS

LIP LINER

LIPSTICK

GLOSS

NOTES / INSPIRATION

KEY PRODUCTS AND TOOLS

CLIENT NAME

DATE

PHONE

EMAIL

LOOK / OCCASION

SKIN

PRIMER

FOUNDATION

CONCEALER

POWDER

HIGHLIGHTER

CONTOUR

BLUSH

EYES

BROW BONE

LID

CREASE

UNDER EYE

EYELINER

MASCARA

BROW

LIPS

LIP LINER

LIPSTICK

GLOSS

KEY PRODUCTS AND TOOLS

NOTES / INSPIRATION

CLIENT NAME

DATE

PHONE

EMAIL

LOOK / OCCASION

SKIN

PRIMER

FOUNDATION

CONCEALER

POWDER

HIGHLIGHTER

CONTOUR

BLUSH

EYES

BROW BONE

LID

CREASE

UNDER EYE

EYELINER

MASCARA

BROW

LIPS

LIP LINER

LIPSTICK

GLOSS

NOTES / INSPIRATION

KEY PRODUCTS AND TOOLS

CLIENT NAME

DATE

PHONE

EMAIL

LOOK / OCCASION

SKIN

PRIMER

FOUNDATION

CONCEALER

POWDER

HIGHLIGHTER

CONTOUR

BLUSH

EYES

BROW BONE

LID

CREASE

UNDER EYE

EYELINER

MASCARA

BROW

LIPS

LIP LINER

LIPSTICK

GLOSS

KEY PRODUCTS AND TOOLS

NOTES / INSPIRATION

CLIENT NAME

DATE

PHONE

EMAIL

LOOK / OCCASION

SKIN

PRIMER

FOUNDATION

CONCEALER

POWDER

HIGHLIGHTER

CONTOUR

BLUSH

EYES

BROW BONE

LID

CREASE

UNDER EYE

EYELINER

MASCARA

BROW

LIPS

LIP LINER

LIPSTICK

GLOSS

NOTES / INSPIRATION

KEY PRODUCTS AND TOOLS

CLIENT NAME

DATE

PHONE

EMAIL

LOOK / OCCASION

SKIN

PRIMER

FOUNDATION

CONCEALER

POWDER

HIGHLIGHTER

CONTOUR

BLUSH

EYES

BROW BONE

LID

CREASE

UNDER EYE

EYELINER

MASCARA

BROW

LIPS

LIP LINER

LIPSTICK

GLOSS

KEY PRODUCTS AND TOOLS

NOTES / INSPIRATION

CLIENT NAME

DATE

PHONE

EMAIL

LOOK / OCCASION

SKIN

PRIMER

FOUNDATION

CONCEALER

POWDER

HIGHLIGHTER

CONTOUR

BLUSH

EYES

BROW BONE

LID

CREASE

UNDER EYE

EYELINER

MASCARA

BROW

LIPS

LIP LINER

LIPSTICK

GLOSS

NOTES / INSPIRATION

KEY PRODUCTS AND TOOLS

CLIENT NAME

DATE

PHONE

EMAIL

LOOK / OCCASION

SKIN

PRIMER

FOUNDATION

CONCEALER

POWDER

HIGHLIGHTER

CONTOUR

BLUSH

EYES

BROW BONE

LID

CREASE

UNDER EYE

EYELINER

MASCARA

BROW

LIPS

LIP LINER

LIPSTICK

GLOSS

KEY PRODUCTS AND TOOLS

NOTES / INSPIRATION

CLIENT NAME

DATE

PHONE

EMAIL

LOOK / OCCASION

SKIN

PRIMER

FOUNDATION

CONCEALER

POWDER

HIGHLIGHTER

CONTOUR

BLUSH

EYES

BROW BONE

LID

CREASE

UNDER EYE

EYELINER

MASCARA

BROW

LIPS

LIP LINER

LIPSTICK

GLOSS

NOTES / INSPIRATION

KEY PRODUCTS AND TOOLS

CLIENT NAME

DATE

PHONE

EMAIL

LOOK / OCCASION

SKIN

PRIMER

FOUNDATION

CONCEALER

POWDER

HIGHLIGHTER

CONTOUR

BLUSH

EYES

BROW BONE

LID

CREASE

UNDER EYE

EYELINER

MASCARA

BROW

LIPS

LIP LINER

LIPSTICK

GLOSS

NOTES / INSPIRATION

KEY PRODUCTS AND TOOLS

CLIENT NAME

DATE

PHONE

EMAIL

LOOK / OCCASION

SKIN

PRIMER

FOUNDATION

CONCEALER

POWDER

HIGHLIGHTER

CONTOUR

BLUSH

EYES

BROW BONE

LID

CREASE

UNDER EYE

EYELINER

MASCARA

BROW

LIPS

LIP LINER

LIPSTICK

GLOSS

KEY PRODUCTS AND TOOLS

NOTES / INSPIRATION

CLIENT NAME

DATE

PHONE

EMAIL

LOOK / OCCASION

SKIN

PRIMER

FOUNDATION

CONCEALER

POWDER

HIGHLIGHTER

CONTOUR

BLUSH

EYES

BROW BONE

LID

CREASE

UNDER EYE

EYELINER

MASCARA

BROW

LIPS

LIP LINER

LIPSTICK

GLOSS

KEY PRODUCTS AND TOOLS

NOTES / INSPIRATION

CLIENT NAME

DATE

PHONE

EMAIL

LOOK / OCCASION

SKIN

PRIMER

FOUNDATION

CONCEALER

POWDER

HIGHLIGHTER

CONTOUR

BLUSH

EYES

BROW BONE

LID

CREASE

UNDER EYE

EYELINER

MASCARA

BROW

LIPS

LIP LINER

LIPSTICK

GLOSS

KEY PRODUCTS AND TOOLS

NOTES / INSPIRATION

CLIENT NAME

DATE

PHONE

EMAIL

LOOK / OCCASION

SKIN

PRIMER

FOUNDATION

CONCEALER

POWDER

HIGHLIGHTER

CONTOUR

BLUSH

EYES

BROW BONE

LID

CREASE

UNDER EYE

EYELINER

MASCARA

BROW

LIPS

LIP LINER

LIPSTICK

GLOSS

KEY PRODUCTS AND TOOLS

NOTES / INSPIRATION

CLIENT NAME

DATE

PHONE

EMAIL

LOOK / OCCASION

SKIN

PRIMER

FOUNDATION

CONCEALER

POWDER

HIGHLIGHTER

CONTOUR

BLUSH

EYES

BROW BONE

LID

CREASE

UNDER EYE

EYELINER

MASCARA

BROW

LIPS

LIP LINER

LIPSTICK

GLOSS

KEY PRODUCTS AND TOOLS

NOTES / INSPIRATION

CLIENT NAME

DATE

PHONE

EMAIL

LOOK / OCCASION

SKIN

PRIMER

FOUNDATION

CONCEALER

POWDER

HIGHLIGHTER

CONTOUR

BLUSH

EYES

BROW BONE

LID

CREASE

UNDER EYE

EYELINER

MASCARA

BROW

LIPS

LIP LINER

LIPSTICK

GLOSS

KEY PRODUCTS AND TOOLS

NOTES / INSPIRATION

CLIENT NAME

DATE

PHONE

EMAIL

LOOK / OCCASION

SKIN

PRIMER

FOUNDATION

CONCEALER

POWDER

HIGHLIGHTER

CONTOUR

BLUSH

EYES

BROW BONE

LID

CREASE

UNDER EYE

EYELINER

MASCARA

BROW

LIPS

LIP LINER

LIPSTICK

GLOSS

KEY PRODUCTS AND TOOLS

NOTES / INSPIRATION

CLIENT NAME

DATE

PHONE

EMAIL

LOOK / OCCASION

SKIN

PRIMER

FOUNDATION

CONCEALER

POWDER

HIGHLIGHTER

CONTOUR

BLUSH

EYES

BROW BONE

LID

CREASE

UNDER EYE

EYELINER

MASCARA

BROW

LIPS

LIP LINER

LIPSTICK

GLOSS

KEY PRODUCTS AND TOOLS

NOTES / INSPIRATION

CLIENT NAME

DATE

PHONE

EMAIL

LOOK / OCCASION

SKIN

PRIMER

FOUNDATION

CONCEALER

POWDER

HIGHLIGHTER

CONTOUR

BLUSH

EYES

BROW BONE

LID

CREASE

UNDER EYE

EYELINER

MASCARA

BROW

LIPS

LIP LINER

LIPSTICK

GLOSS

NOTES / INSPIRATION

KEY PRODUCTS AND TOOLS

CLIENT NAME

DATE

PHONE

EMAIL

LOOK / OCCASION

SKIN

PRIMER

FOUNDATION

CONCEALER

POWDER

HIGHLIGHTER

CONTOUR

BLUSH

EYES

BROW BONE

LID

CREASE

UNDER EYE

EYELINER

MASCARA

BROW

LIPS

LIP LINER

LIPSTICK

GLOSS

KEY PRODUCTS AND TOOLS

NOTES / INSPIRATION

CLIENT NAME

DATE

PHONE

EMAIL

LOOK / OCCASION

SKIN

PRIMER

FOUNDATION

CONCEALER

POWDER

HIGHLIGHTER

CONTOUR

BLUSH

EYES

BROW BONE

LID

CREASE

UNDER EYE

EYELINER

MASCARA

BROW

LIPS

LIP LINER

LIPSTICK

GLOSS

KEY PRODUCTS AND TOOLS

NOTES / INSPIRATION

CLIENT NAME

DATE

PHONE

EMAIL

LOOK / OCCASION

SKIN

PRIMER

FOUNDATION

CONCEALER

POWDER

HIGHLIGHTER

CONTOUR

BLUSH

EYES

BROW BONE

LID

CREASE

UNDER EYE

EYELINER

MASCARA

BROW

LIPS

LIP LINER

LIPSTICK

GLOSS

NOTES / INSPIRATION

KEY PRODUCTS AND TOOLS

CLIENT NAME

DATE

PHONE

EMAIL

LOOK / OCCASION

SKIN

PRIMER

FOUNDATION

CONCEALER

POWDER

HIGHLIGHTER

CONTOUR

BLUSH

EYES

BROW BONE

LID

CREASE

UNDER EYE

EYELINER

MASCARA

BROW

LIPS

LIP LINER

LIPSTICK

GLOSS

KEY PRODUCTS AND TOOLS

NOTES / INSPIRATION

CLIENT NAME

DATE

PHONE

EMAIL

LOOK / OCCASION

SKIN

PRIMER

FOUNDATION

CONCEALER

POWDER

HIGHLIGHTER

CONTOUR

BLUSH

EYES

BROW BONE

LID

CREASE

UNDER EYE

EYELINER

MASCARA

BROW

LIPS

LIP LINER

LIPSTICK

GLOSS

NOTES / INSPIRATION

KEY PRODUCTS AND TOOLS

CLIENT NAME

DATE

PHONE

EMAIL

LOOK / OCCASION

SKIN

PRIMER

FOUNDATION

CONCEALER

POWDER

HIGHLIGHTER

CONTOUR

BLUSH

EYES

BROW BONE

LID

CREASE

UNDER EYE

EYELINER

MASCARA

BROW

LIPS

LIP LINER

LIPSTICK

GLOSS

KEY PRODUCTS AND TOOLS

NOTES / INSPIRATION

116

CLIENT NAME

DATE

PHONE

EMAIL

LOOK / OCCASION

SKIN

PRIMER

FOUNDATION

CONCEALER

POWDER

HIGHLIGHTER

CONTOUR

BLUSH

EYES

BROW BONE

LID

CREASE

UNDER EYE

EYELINER

MASCARA

BROW

LIPS

LIP LINER

LIPSTICK

GLOSS

KEY PRODUCTS AND TOOLS

NOTES / INSPIRATION

CLIENT NAME

DATE

PHONE

EMAIL

LOOK / OCCASION

SKIN

PRIMER

FOUNDATION

CONCEALER

POWDER

HIGHLIGHTER

CONTOUR

BLUSH

EYES

BROW BONE

LID

CREASE

UNDER EYE

EYELINER

MASCARA

BROW

LIPS

LIP LINER

LIPSTICK

GLOSS

KEY PRODUCTS AND TOOLS

NOTES / INSPIRATION

Made in the USA
Las Vegas, NV
02 January 2024

83800582R00070